Y0-AQV-215

GOD
AT
MY
ELBOW

Harold F. Leestma

GOD
AT
MY
ELBOW

The Meaning of Conversion

WORD BOOKS, Publisher
Waco, Texas

PARK CITY BAPTIST CHURCH
PARK CITY, KENTUCKY

GOD AT MY ELBOW
Copyright © 1972 by Word, Incorporated
Waco, Texas 76703

All rights reserved. No part of this book may be reproduced in any form without permission from the publisher except for brief quotations in reviews.

Quotations from the Revised Standard Version of the Bible, copyright 1946 and 1952 by the Division of Christian Education of the National Council of Churches of Christ in the United States of America, used by permission; the Today's English Version of the New Testament, copyright © American Bible Society, 1966; The New English Bible © The Delegates of The Oxford University Press and The Syndics of The Cambridge University Press, 1961, 1970, reprinted by permission; The Living New Testament © 1967 by Tyndale House Publishers, Wheaton, Illinois. Unless otherwise noted Scriptures are from the King James Version.

Library of Congress catalog card number: 72-84165
Printed in the United States of America

With love and gratitude

to

Lois, my wife,

who, by her constant encouragement,

her love that never fails,

and her daily walk with God,

helped me write this book

CONTENTS

FOREWORD

A few years ago I conducted a preaching-teaching-reaching mission at a church in New Jersey. The pastor had made preparation by enlisting a number of couples who were willing to make calls on unchurched families in the community. I taught three training sessions on "How to Share Your Faith," explaining the naturalness of the Christian witness and how to help people turn in a new direction and find a new life in Christ. One of the points I emphasized was that God is with us always—*God is at your elbow!*

On Sunday afternoon we met for a final motivating prayer session and then were ready to go out to make our calls. Just before we left the room, one man raised his hand, and I acknowledged him. All he said was, "I'm scared!" I said, "All of us are scared," and once again emphasized the fact that *God is at your elbow.*

When the teams returned to report on their calls, this man and his wife had a most interesting story to tell. When they reached their car, which was parked in the church parking lot, the husband claimed that he had left his keys in the church. Later he "discovered" them in his pocket, but he knew they were there all the time. They started out, and he turned the wrong way at the first intersection. His wife soon realized that he was afraid and persuaded him to go down the correct street. As they passed the house where they were to

9

make their first call, he said, "I'm sure no one's home," although through the window they could see people seated in the living room. Finally, they turned around and parked in front of the house. As they stood on the porch, they remembered that they had not agreed on who was to lead the interview.

He said quickly to her, "You talk first."

She said, "Then, you ring the doorbell."

He related to us how difficult it was for him to do this—his right arm just would not move. He looked at his wife standing at his left. He tried to move his arm and nothing happened.

Suddenly, his arm went forward and his finger pressed the doorbell. The thought flashed through his mind—*God is at my elbow*—and he quickly turned to see if someone was standing there.

The door opened; his wife began the conversation, and the two of them entered the home. This unchurched couple was just waiting for someone to show them Christian love and concern. They were present at the evening service, and both came forward when I gave the invitation to surrender to Christ.

In the following chapters I want to share with you the certainty that Jesus Christ is alive, performing modern-day miracles, turning people from darkness to light, from loneliness to fellowship, from selfishness to salvation, from despair to faith, from defeat to victory, and from chaos to Christ.

God loves you and he is with you always!

HAROLD F. LEESTMA

10

A COMPLETE TURN

Conversion

THIS PAST WEEK I traveled to various parts of the country; in a Florida church I observed methods of evangelism, in New York City I attended a denominational board meeting. Coming back to California, I stopped in Dallas, then went on to a delightful little town also in Texas. There I met such unassuming, neighborly people. Everyone I encountered had a cordial spirit. "What can I do for you?" was a common question.

On a balmy evening I went for a long walk to the edge of town, then decided to return to my motel by a different route. I walked to a service station to check out what other way there might be and found the manager of that station standing in the doorway talking to an attractive, clean-cut boy about twelve years old.

The station manager asked me what I wanted and showed me the best route back to my motel. Then he added, "You know, this young fellow here has two jack-knives, and he wants me to buy them for a dollar. I think maybe I will. He's been offered a quarter, but he says he thinks he can get more than that for them. So he wants to sell these two knives to me for a dollar. Do you think they're worth it?"

I looked at the boy. I said, "It all depends on what he is going to do with the money. . . . Son, what are you going to do with that dollar?"

He said, "Well, there's a pair of boots in that store." He pointed to a shoe store across the street. "They cost ten dollars, but I've been talking to the owner; and he

13

says if I pay a dollar every week until I bring in eight dollars, I can have the boots."

I asked, "How far are you?"

He said seriously, "I'm up to four dollars."

The boy was trying to earn a dollar a week, and this week he was trying to sell these two jackknives—one pretty rusty and the other a souvenir of some lumber company!

I said to the station manager, "Do you know, friend, I think they're worth a dollar apiece, to tell you the truth!" We looked at each other. I took a dollar out of my billfold, and he did the same. We handed two dollars to that little fellow. He thanked us with feeling and ran across the street into that shoe store, to put down two more dollars toward the eight dollars on the ten-dollar boots.

I've been thinking about that boy. He wasn't expecting all that! After someone offered him twenty-five cents, I'm sure he thought he wouldn't be able to increase that by much more than a dime. But he asked for a dollar anyway, and all of a sudden he had *two* dollars toward something he wanted very, very much.

Often people come to God, not really expecting a great deal from him, and then suddenly the words of the Old Testament prophet become a reality: *"I will . . . open the windows of heaven for you and pour down for you an overflowing blessing"* (Mal. 3:10, RSV).

When a man turns from the old life
    into the new life in Christ,

14

A Complete Turn

    when his life is turned around
      in a new direction,
blessings come pouring in,
and he receives more than he ever expected.
Jesus Christ offers us himself,
not in any small measure.
When we open our hearts and minds
we may expect big things from God!

This whole matter of turning around, or conversion, is defined in the New Testament: *"Truly, I say to you, unless you turn and become like children, you will never enter the kingdom of heaven"* (Matt. 18:3, RSV).

The great Hindu poet and philosopher Tagore called this the most beautiful verse in the whole Bible.

Except you turn around,
    and your life is changed,
      and you go in his direction,
        there will be no entrance to the
        kingdom of God for you.
The conversion is the root,
    and the kingdom of God is the fruit.

What does it really mean to be converted?
It means to turn in a new direction,
    to turn your back on Satan,
      and to set your face toward the Savior.
Ask yourself,

"Is my face, or my back, toward Jesus Christ?"
Turn from the low,
        the selfish,
           the cheap,
              the wrong.
Turn to the high,
        the noble,
           the clean,
              the right.

Conversion means
        TO TURN AROUND,
but it carries with it this meaning:
        TO TURN WITH.
The decision to turn around is your decision, but the
partnership and the help with which to do it is from
God.

God helps you to make the break,
   but the decision must be yours.
Then, when you make this decision,
   you discover he is there,
      helping you change your direction.
Conversion means turning with him.
And what does it mean to "become as little children"?
It means
        TO BE RECEPTIVE.
A child is receptive;
   he accepts what you hand him.

A Complete Turn

Whether you give him your hand,
  your smile,
    food,
      or a toy,
        he trusts you.
The child's major attitude is receptivity.
He'll take; he'll receive.

When you are converted, you look trustingly into the
  face of the Father,
and you are receptive.
  You accept what he gives
  because you trust him.
Since it is his voice, you listen.
  Since it is his hand, you take it.
    Whether he leads over a hill or through a valley,
    you willingly walk his way.

Conversion also means
  A NEW ATMOSPHERE OF LIVING
because now you are in the kingdom of God. Maybe
the circumstances will not change, but you will change.
Maybe the attitude of someone toward you will not
change, but your attitude toward that person will
change.
  You will have a new motive,
    a new goal,
      a new spirit,
        a new outlook.

17

God says, "Turn my way."
  I say, "I am willing."
God says, "I will help you."
  I say, "I know I need you."
God says, "Will you trust me, my child?"
  I say, "Yes, Father."
God says, "Now you are in my kingdom."
  I answer exuberantly,
    "A NEW LIFE IS MINE!
      I am released . . . receptive . . . relaxed.
      I have made a complete turn."

Some people turn toward Jesus Christ because they are impressed by things they see and hear. They look, they gaze, they are awed even, but they hesitate to make a complete commitment. They begin to turn to him but don't follow through.

SOME STOP WITH BEING IMPRESSED.

Think of the wise men from the East. They came a long distance across deserts to see a newborn king. They saw him in a house in Bethlehem. They were awed by this, impressed by it, and they gave their gifts. Then they went away, and there is no record of a Christian movement at that time in Persia. I think the wise men were very much impressed, but we do not read that they committed themselves in complete loyalty to this new King of Kings.

A Complete Turn

People are impressed by the church and sometimes awed by it. They see the thousands of worshiping people. They see the beautiful buildings. They catch something of the contagion of enthusiasm and joy, and the positive power of the gospel for modern man. They are impressed with the greatness of our God. And yet, not all step forward to find new life and come into the kingdom.

Some people don't make a full turn and enter the kingdom because, as Stanley Jones once described it,

SOME GET CONVERTED TO THE CONVERTER.

A New Testament example of that concerns the followers of John the Baptist. He was a great preacher. People came many miles to hear him. They listened very intently. Soon the narrator uses the phrase, "the disciples of John . . . the disciples of John." Do you know that there is a movement in Iraq called the Disciples of John the Baptist? These people have their own sacred writings, called the Ginza. Each year every member of that movement must be baptized again in a white robe. But they have never become Christian. They're still followers of John the Baptist.

Don't blame John for that. He never tried to gather around himself "the disciples of John." One day, when he saw Jesus walking over a hill toward them, John said to his disciples, *"Look! There is the Lamb of God who takes away the world's sin"* (John 1:29 b, LNT). *"He*

19

must increase, but I must decrease" (John 3:30, RSV).

Some people never got further than following John. They never looked beyond him to see Jesus.

At the Billy Graham Crusade in Anaheim Stadium, I stood on the playing field every night and tried to help people find their way to Jesus Christ. The second evening of the crusade, a young fellow came forward and stood next to me. He said he had driven that afternoon from a college in San Bernardino. I asked him, "Why did you come here tonight?"

He said, "Well, I don't know, really. I've heard a lot about Billy Graham, but I had never heard or seen him first-hand, and I just wanted to come and see and hear him."

Then he turned his eyes away from me and looked up at Billy, who was still standing on the platform. He said, "He's really something."

Now, I wouldn't detract from that for one minute. But it was my assignment under God to help this young man look beyond the converter to the Christ that Graham wanted him to see.

After some conversation together, I said, "Now, let's pray." I put my hands on his shoulders, and he put his hands on my shoulders. We bowed our heads—our heads were touching—and first I prayed, for him. Then he prayed a very simple prayer.

He said, "Thank you, God, for Billy Graham. Thank you for this man that I just met. And thank you for Jesus Christ; I'm really going to try to follow him. Amen."

20

A Complete Turn

I was truly thankful to God! I felt this young man had gone beyond the converter—to the Christ.

Another reason some people don't go far enough and turn all the way to Christ is that

SOME STILL HAVE A FEW RESERVATIONS.

It's significant that when Jesus called some men to follow him one of them said, *"Let me first say good-bye to my people at home"* (Luke 9:61 b, NEB).

I think Jesus must have looked that man straight in the eye and said, "Look, my friend, put first things first. I asked you to come follow me now—no reservations, none at all."

This wonderful,
  matchless,
    loving,
      living Christ
invites us to come to him,
and often we say,
  "I would follow you,
    but . . ."
But what?
What could it be
  that's held in reserve,
    that has higher priority,
      before we really step out
        and give ourselves away to him?
Put first things first!
Follow him now—with no reservations!

In the *Los Angeles Times* I read an item about Chad Everett, star of the television series "Medical Center." During the fire in Los Angeles some time ago, he was working on the set. From there he could smell the smoke and see the yellow glow in the afternoon sky.

He told a newspaper reporter, "My wife called and said the smoke was about two hundred and fifty yards from our home. I told her, 'Get out! Get out with the baby—the dog—anything else that's alive—and never mind the rest!' "

Then he said, "When I was driving home on the freeway that night, I heard the news announcer say that my home had been destroyed by fire."

Only fifteen minutes after his wife Shelby grabbed the baby and called the dog, there was an explosion in that house from all the heat. Concrete, steel, and a tile roof were gone. Forty-six hundred feet of housing gone in five minutes.

Now, here's what Chad Everett added: "During that weekend, a lot of us who were burned out were sitting around in a restaurant, talking. My little daughter Carrie was in my arms. She looked at me, and suddenly she put her arms around me, took my big face in her little hands, and then kissed me all over my face. . . . What do stone and tile and lumber matter compared to this?"

First things first! And in the one life we have to live I believe that Jesus Christ is first.

Finally, some may be almost converted because they

are depending on the faith of someone else, not their own faith.

SOME TRY TO LIVE ON A SECONDHAND POWER.

A meaningful New Testament story that relates to this is from the Book of Acts, the nineteenth chapter. Some traveling entertainers noticed that Saint Paul had a large following. So these itinerants went to see and to hear him. They saw that Paul, by the power of God, was healing some people's bodies and minds. All around him were transformed people. The itinerant magicians decided to try a healing ministry, too.

They tried it with a person whom the New Testament described as "possessed with a demon." The leader of the group said, "By the Jesus whom Paul preaches, I order you to be healed!"

Nothing happened.

Of course not! It was secondhand. There was no power there. He was using quotation marks, instead of the real thing. The "secondhand" became "second-rate."

You can't live on the faith of someone else . . .

    not on the faith of your parents,

      not on the faith of a preacher,

        not on the faith of your wife or your husband,

        not on the faith of your friend.

It has to be your own faith.

When you accept Christ
   as your personal Redeemer,
      then the inexhaustible,
         invincible resources of God
            become your own.
Firsthand power is available.
Our Lord will give you everything you need!

Parent, teacher, pastoral counselor, Christian doctor, and psychiatrist, you all know this. Often those who come to you for help or who ask for advice or counsel will pour out their story. Finally they'll say to you, the counselor, "Well, if I had your faith, or if I had your enthusiasm, or if I had your joy . . ."

The wise counselor will say, "I'm glad to share my faith with you, glad to share my enthusiasm and my joy, but this faith has to become *your* faith."

The sun is ninety-three million miles away from this earth. I have read that if the sun were to move an infinitesimal fraction of its distance nearer to our earth every living thing would be scorched and burned alive! And if the sun were to move an infinitesimal fraction of its distance away from our earth, this whole planet would be covered with thick, solid ice, destroying everything. What a difference one small change would make!

Are you too far away from God?
What a difference one step could make!
It may be just one small step for you,

24

A Complete Turn

but it could be the giant step of your life . . .
   a step in God's direction,
      a step with him,
      your own step of faith
      that says, "I'll take him."
Take the step,
   not a half-step,
      not a half-turn,
         but the whole turn,
            and with no reservations.
He'll take you just as you are!
   He loves you,
      he wants you,
         he'll help you.
Come . . . and tell him,
   "I want to be
   100 percent
   yours!"

         Father,
            I'm convinced that
            being almost converted is not enough.
            I want to be 100 percent yours.
               I know you love me.
               I know you want me.
               I know you'll help me.
            THIS IS MY TURNING POINT.
            Christ is mine forever!
               Amen

GOING IN GOD'S DIRECTION

Jacob

The greatest need for any man in the world
   at any time
is to get his life changed,
   to be turned around,
     transformed,
       converted,
         made into the likeness of Christ,
to go, not in his own selfish direction
   but in God's direction.
Such a person's life expands.
He becomes an exemplary person.
He's full of joy,
        exhilaration,
         enthusiasm,
and he discovers before long that
this new life is not only abundant,
but it is everlasting!
This change is possible. It is happening to people,
day after day, all over the world.

People who have been moving in the wrong direction
are discovering that God takes the initiative,
and they respond in faith
and move in a new direction!
The initiative is God's; the response is ours.

I'm thankful that God took the initiative in my life
and let me discover how he wanted me to go and where
he wanted me to go. The biggest problem was *when*,

but he kept insisting on it, and finally I surrendered. It's been a new life, a good life, a wonderful life, a beautiful life. I wouldn't trade it for any other, I assure you. It's the only way I ever want to go—Christ's Way —and I want to do everything I can for the rest of my life to help people go his Way.

New life often comes suddenly and dramatically. Sometimes it develops gradually. It's real, either way. What matters is that you are going the Way—Christ's Way.

A sign on a hotel door said, "If this door seems to be locked, just turn the knob." As simple as that!

If a door into the new life
   seems to be locked,
      turn the knob.
         Turn the knob called faith!

New life consists of a series of two steps: CRISIS and PROCESS.

Conversion is the crisis of meeting God and turning in his direction. The new life that follows is the process of growing into his likeness.

In genuine conversion there is no conflict between the mind and the heart. There will no longer be a division between how a man feels about God and what he thinks about God. These two aspects of conversion belong together, in the total person. Knowing and feeling are joined together in a beautiful harmony.

30

Going in God's Direction

So, when a man responds to God, he doesn't have to have all his questions answered, nor does he have to have a cataclysmic emotional feeling. What is important is that, with both mind and spirit, a man stands up and takes God at his word.

One morning I was on the patio and happened to see our daughter Mary there. She was carrying her baby boy, Scott. Scott was looking backward over her shoulder. All that Mary said was, "Scott, turn around and see grandpa!" And he did. He put out his arms, and so did I, and there I was, holding him. What a very nice feeling to hold him, as we love to do!

It reminded me that a lot of people are insecure and missing the abundant life. How simple it would be to turn around and discover that Christ is right there, waiting for you.

Turn around, and there he stands,
  arms outstretched,
    waiting to take you
      and make you his own.
Just turn around
  and you'll find yourself
    in the arms of redeeming love.

A lot of people make just a start in the right direction. I want to tell you about a Bible character who did this. The largest share of his life concerned his moving toward full conversion. His name, Jacob, means deceiver.

He cheated his brother. He deceived his aged father. He tricked his uncle. Even though he had a religious atmosphere around him, he had never given himself to God. Jacob kept *himself* at the center rather than God. Jacob always looked after Jacob!

When his brother Esau was terribly hungry after a long hunting trip and came home saying, "I'm starving," Jacob took advantage of him. He made his brother Esau give him his birthright in exchange for a hot meal. Then he schemed a clever plot with his mother against his father.

He got what was coming to him—his brother's hatred. Jacob had to run. He ran from Esau, over hills, across plains, and through valleys.

Exhausted and terribly afraid, with a stone for a pillow, he lay down at night to sleep. In a dream, he saw a ladder reaching from earth to heaven and angels of God going up and down the ladder. At the top was God.

When Jacob woke up, he said, *"Surely the Lord is in this place; and I did not know it. . . . This is . . . the house of God"* (Gen. 28:16, 17, rsv).

He was deeply moved by his experience, and he decided that he would make a promise to God. When you read this promise, you'll see a man who made only a half-turn although at the first reading it sounds as if Jacob were wonderfully devout.

Jacob made a vow, saying, *"If God will be with me, and will keep me in this way that I go, and will give*

*me bread to eat and clothing to wear, so that I come
again to my father's house in peace, then the Lord shall
be my God"* (Gen. 28:20, 21, RSV).

HE TRIED TO MAKE A DEAL WITH GOD.

"And this stone which I have set up for a pillar shall
be God's house—if God is good to me."

After that, he promised, "And of all that you give
me, God, I will give a tenth to you." Notice: Jacob was
willing to give a tenth, but he didn't give *himself!* Jacob
kept himself for himself.

God isn't going to give up on a man like that, but
something more will have to happen.

Jacob had all the outward appearances
    of being religious,
        but Jacob had to give himself. . . .
That's the only "deal" God will ever make!

Jacob kept himself at the center of his life. For four-
teen years he worked for his uncle Laban, and all the
time he worked he was scheming, rationalizing his dis-
honesty, dividing his life into the compartments of
secular and sacred.

He got his way, he got his wealth, and then he got
his payoff. Once again, run for your life, Jacob! For
now Uncle Laban and all of his servants were after him.

With an inward fear,

33

with a false center,
with an emptiness inside,

HE RAN FOR A LONG TIME—

until one night he wrestled it out with God.

God and Jacob wrestled through the night. God was determined to turn him all the way. God asked him a question: *"What is your name?"* (Gen. 32:27, RSV).

That's an important question. It was especially important in those days when names were associated with the character of a man.

Jacob said, "My name is Jacob, the deceiver, the treacherous one, the low-natured."

That was the honest moment of Jacob's life. That was the moment of truth!

"What is your name?"
"I am a deceiver. . . .
I am wrong. . . .
I need help."

Now Jacob had turned with *both* his mind and heart.

Then God said to Jacob, "I'll give you a new name. I'll turn you around and I'll call you 'Israel,' which means 'striver with God,' because you have had a wrestling with me tonight and the victory has been won."

34

NOW HE WAS A NEW MAN—
WITH A NEW NAME!

All those restless years, all that time of emptiness, and all that ineffectiveness, scheming, and plotting—those years were gone. Jacob couldn't relive them. If he had only made a full turn long ago!

Have you made the full turn?
Or just half a turn?
  No deals,
    just one requirement:
      give up *yourself*,
        surrender to Christ!

What is your name?
Is your name Ego?
  Is your name Fear?
    Is your name Self-Pity?
      Is your name Loneliness?
      Is your name Guilt?

YOU CAN HAVE YOUR NAME CHANGED!

If your name is Ego, it can be changed to Christian—
  no longer self-centered, but God-centered!
If your name is Fear, it can be changed to Faith.
If your name is Self-Pity, it can be changed to
  Confidence through Christ.

If your name is Loneliness, it can be changed to
Friendship!
If your name is Guilt, it can be changed to For-
giveness!

Just turn around
in his direction,
and you'll discover a wholeness,
a completeness to life,
as you turn to the open arms
of Christ's redeeming love.

God,
I'm thankful you never give up.
Where there are areas of my life
not yet surrendered,
I surrender now.
I NOW HAVE A NEW DIRECTION, A NEW NAME—
because you love me.
Thank you, Father!
Amen

CONVERTED FROM DOUBT TO FAITH

Thomas

A LITTLE BOY stood next to his father, who was sitting in a chair. The little boy said, "Look, daddy! I'm taller than you are." As long as his daddy was sitting in that chair, he was. Of course, when daddy stood up, the boy was not as tall.

There's a man described in the New Testament who's a very likable person. We find ourselves relating to him very easily. He's called by most people "Doubting Thomas." That's an unfair description, I think, of a very noble man. When we think of Thomas, we feel like the little boy standing next to his father.

We feel so much taller than Thomas
  in his doubts,
    his hesitations,
      and his fears. . . .
But look at the man when he stands up!
We find him standing
  with the dignity of a great faith,
    a personal surrender to Jesus Christ,
      a great achievement in his life,
and we learn a little more about our own stature.

Thomas was one of the Twelve—the twelve specially chosen apostles.

These men worked with Jesus,
  lived with Jesus,
    listened to what he said,

39

watched his miracles,
and saw the tremendous potential
there was in this new movement.

One time Jesus said, "I'm going to Jerusalem."

Some of the disciples said, "No, no, it won't be good for you to go there; the opposition is too strong."

Thomas said, "Let's go!" "*Let us also go, that we may die with him*" (John 11:16).

He was a man of courage! He knew what to do. Ready to go, unafraid.

In John 20, the story seems to portray a different person, but he isn't really different at all. Here is the same man, but now he finds it very difficult to believe that Jesus Christ has come back from the dead, that he's alive, really alive. Thomas saw him crucified. Thomas knew they laid him in a grave! And—he's alive? . . . Alive?

He's not an agnostic, just hesitant and practical. He shakes his head and says, quietly but firmly, "Until I see in his hands the print of the nails, and put my hand on that spear-thrust in his side, I just—I just can't believe it, men. I just can't see it." That was Thomas in his doubt.

You see, the first night after the resurrection, the disciples all went to that upper room where they often met with Jesus. But not Thomas, and not Judas this time. Just ten of them were there that night. And Jesus came and said, "*Peace be with you. . . . Receive the Holy Spirit*" (John 20:21, 22, RSV).

40

Converted from Doubt to Faith

They went out, transformed—
    changed men!
        And they shared their Good News
        with their brother Thomas,
        who had been absent
        and had missed this blessing.
They didn't keep it to themselves. . . .
        "Where's Thomas?"
With deep concern, they went to share their faith.
        "Thomas, we've seen him!
        He's alive!"
        "We have seen the Lord" (John 20:25, RSV).

He could see that something in these men was different. Something had happened, something was changed.

If it hadn't been for the glowing witness
    of those radiant men sharing their faith,
        would Thomas ever have found his Savior at all?
That's our business, too—sharing our faith:
"He is here—we have seen him!"

One night a week later, Thomas was with his friends in the upper room, the doors were shut, and Jesus came. He said again, "Peace be with you."

Then he said directly to Thomas, "Thomas, look. Look at the nail prints in my hands. Here, touch the side where the spear was. Don't be a doubter. Believe, Thomas, believe. . . . Trust me."

In that moment
   an overwhelming faith came to Thomas, .
    flooding his whole life,
     and kneeling before Jesus, he said,
      "My Lord and my God!"

The rest of the story tells that this believer became an achiever.

Legend says that when Jesus went away into heaven his disciples divided the world, saying, "We'll take our choices, make our plans, and then we'll go into different parts of the world."

The lot fell to Thomas to go to India, and he didn't want to go. He said, "I'm not strong enough. I'm not healthy enough to stand the climate. Besides, I'm a Hebrew, and the Indian people won't listen to me . . . and . . . I just don't want to go there."

Then Jesus spoke to him in a vision: "Fear not, Thomas. Go to India and preach the word there, and I will be with you."

Still he refused. That's like him—a bit stubborn at first.

The legend continues. Thomas dreamed that a certain merchant from India came to Jerusalem. His name was Abanes. Abanes had been sent by King Gundiphorus to find a skilled carpenter and bring him back to India to build a beautiful palace. Now Thomas was an expert carpenter.

In the dream Thomas saw this man Abanes in the

marketplace, looking for a carpenter. He saw Jesus meeting Abanes. Jesus said to Abanes, "Would you like to buy a carpenter?"

Abanes said, "Yes, that's what I'm here for."

Jesus said, "I have a slave who's a carpenter. I'd like to sell him," and he pointed to Thomas. So they agreed on a price; Thomas was sold. The agreement ran like this: "I, Jesus, the son of Joseph the carpenter, acknowledge that I have sold my slave Thomas unto thee, Abanes, merchant of Gundiphorus, king of India."

After the deed was drawn up, Jesus found Thomas and took him to Abanes. Abanes said, "Is this your master?"

Thomas answered, "He is."

Abanes said, "I have bought you from him." And, in the dream, Thomas said nothing.

But the next morning he rose from his sleep with the dream fresh on his mind; and on his knees he said, "I'll go wherever you want me to go, Jesus. Your will be done."

It's the same Thomas.
A little slow to believe,
a little hesitant,
but once he made up his mind and was certain, he went all the way.

There's a sequel to that story. The legend says that when King Gundiphorus met Thomas he was pleased with him and gave him the commission to build the palace. He gave him lots of money, and Thomas was to go out, buy materials, and build the palace.

But instead when Thomas saw all the starving people, he bought food and clothing for them, and he made shelters for them. Then he went back and got even more money from the king, and all the while the king thought he was using it to build the palace!

When the king asked him about it one day, Thomas said, "Yes, the palace is rising steadily."

After some months, the king became suspicious. He said, "Thomas, have you built the palace for me?"

Thomas answered, "Yes."

"Then when can I go and see it?"

Thomas said, "You cannot see it now. But when you depart this life, then you'll see it." He quoted the words of his master: *"Inasmuch as ye have done it unto one of the least of these . . . , ye have done it unto me"* (Matt. 25:40). *"Lay up for yourselves treasures in heaven"* (Matt. 6:20).

It almost cost Thomas his life, but eventually the king became a Christian.

So much for the traditional legend. Let's shift forward to the man of today. Many people we meet these days are much like our hero Thomas. Many doubt at first and have questions. I find that the questions that people are asking about faith are not mainly of an academic nature.

Very few people are asking, "Is there a God?"

44

They're asking, "Is this God relevant?"
Not "What does it mean to have faith?"
  but "Does this faith work?"
Instead of "Does God hear prayers?"
  it's "If I pray, will it work for me—will he answer?"
They aren't asking whether Jesus Christ can forgive
  and be a strong power in their life.
They're saying, "What if I surrender my life to him?
  Where will it lead me?"
They are asking if Christianity works: the relevant, down-to-earth, practical sort of questions. I think that was Thomas's approach.

He was the man who wanted to put his finger on it,
  to be sure that it worked—
    the "fingertip faith."

HE HAD TO SEE THAT FAITH IS WORKABLE.

Well, that's all right. If a man has questions and says, "I've got to see it work. I've got to see it right here, laid out scientifically and logically," that's all right. God is scientific—and God is logical. Why should we be afraid of that?

If a man wants to see God in the material,
  this is a God-created world,
    and he can find him there!
God speaks through all the tiny details of his world.

45

Thomas had doubts in his mind because

HE GOT OUT OF FELLOWSHIP.

That was a mistake. He thought he could go it alone.

Sometimes, when you're discouraged or disheartened or wondering about things, you'd like to be alone. That's all right; but don't stay there alone. You may need a friend or some counselor to whom you should speak and share your doubts. Perhaps you need the family circle where you can just open up and say how you feel.

Maybe you need a little wider circle—some small sharing group, people whom you trust, and who trust you. You can speak there of the hesitancy of your life, the wonderment of it, the bewilderment of it, or the depression of it.

Thomas had absented himself from the place where the men always met.

In that upper room they prayed,
    they shared,
        they talked,
            they listened.
But Thomas wasn't there,
so his doubts grew.

I like Thomas for this, though:

HE WAS HONEST ABOUT HIS DOUBT.

He didn't say he believed, when he didn't.
  He didn't say, "I understand," when he couldn't.
    He didn't say, "It's all very clear," when it
    wasn't.
He said it like it was,
just the way he felt it:
  "I don't get it. . . .
  I can't accept it. . . .
    I don't see it. . . .
      It can't be!"
Sometimes that kind of doubt
is the step to a real certainty.

That's how it was with Thomas.
Further, I love Thomas because

HE WENT ALL THE WAY TO CERTAINTY.

When he became sure, he was really sure. He exclaimed with no doubt at all, *"My Lord and my God!"* (John 20:28).

In that phrase, he said something that we need to say over and over again. Do you realize that this was the first time Jesus had ever been called God in the New Testament? He had been called Master and Teacher and "Friend." . . . Peter came closer when he said, "You are the Son of the living God."

But Thomas said, "My God."

Yes, Jesus is God.

47

And the word *Lord* is Thomas saying, "I've been on my own now for a few days, and it isn't very healthy out there. I had a real hurt inside of me. I couldn't find my way. But I want to be mastered by the Master. I want to surrender to you. You handle me, you take me. . . . You're the Lord of my life from now on!"

Then he could go marching triumphantly on to do a great work. He built the church of Mar Thoma in south India, which today has four hundred thousand believers—an evangelical church on fire for Christ. Well, that was Thomas. . . . He went from doubt to faith, and on from belief to achievement.

> Wouldn't you like to take the steps
> to a faith that is certain and sure—
> out of any hesitations or uncertainties,
> into the realm where you can say
> clearly and plainly
> to Jesus Christ,
> *"My Lord and my God!"*

Recently I had a phone call from a man who had been a member of our church before he moved away more than a year ago. He told me, "I've settled things now, and I want to go into full-time Christian service of some kind in the church."

I remember so well about a year ago when he came in to see me. His story is in my book, *An Earthling's Walk with God.* He was depressed and discouraged

48

about his job, himself, and his spiritual life. Everything seemed to be going wrong.

He sat in my office, burdened with all of it. A few times in our conversation he told me how, sometimes, he had felt close to God in the services of worship. I suggested to him that he leave the office and sit in the sanctuary all by himself.

"Nobody's there. Just sit in the pew and think it through, and pray to God. Maybe you'll find him there. And then, come back."

He was gone about twenty minutes, and then he came bounding back. My secretary will never forget it. What a difference between the way he went out of that office and the way he came back!

Then he told me how he had sat in the front row for a little while. Finally he had said, "All right, God, I'll give you what you want. I've got it right here. I know it's what you want. And if I give it to you, then I'm expecting you to get me through this, and give me a new life."

He walked from the pew and knelt in front of the cross. He told me that it seemed as if God were saying to him, "All right, what is it you want to give?"

He said, "I'm ready to give it. It isn't much, Lord. It isn't much at all, but I'll give it to you."

God said to him, "Go ahead and give it. What is it?"

He said, "It's me, Lord, . . . just me. That's all.

And God said, "That's what I've been waiting for; I'll take it!"

Out of the shadows,
    wondering,
        depressed,
            uncertain,
                he moved into the light and said,
    "Lord, I'll give you all I've got.
    It isn't much . . . just me."

That is what Thomas did.
In that personal confrontation
    he looked up into Jesus' eyes
        and said, "My Lord and my God,"
            and he came bounding back with a new life!

Let me suggest some steps from hesitancy to certainty.

PUT YOURSELF IN A PLACE WHERE GOD CAN FIND YOU.

The whole story of the New Testament is not one of man trying to find God. . . .
    It's the story of God's search for man,
        of the Good Shepherd
            finding the lost sheep
                and bringing it home.
    You don't have to search for God.
    He's searching for *you*.
    But don't run away.

Converted *from Doubt to Faith*

The second step is to

TURN TOWARD HIM IN AN ATTITUDE OF EXPECTANCY.

He has made promises. The Bible is filled with them: *"He will give his angels charge of you"* (Ps. 91:11, RSV). *"My God will supply every need of yours"* (Phil. 4:19, RSV). *"My grace is sufficient for you"* (2 Cor. 12:9, RSV). *"I came that they may have life"* (John 10:10, RSV).

Just move to him
    with an air of expectancy:
        "Lord, I expect something to happen—now."
        And it will!

Then, of course,

BELIEVE THAT HE'S WITH YOU ALL THE TIME.

Believe that he's with you *right now*. Say some of these reassuring phrases throughout the day:
    "God loves me. . . .
        God is at my elbow. . . .
            God is holding my hand. . . .
                God is looking into my eyes. . . .
                    Jesus Christ is here,
                        he's alive,
                            he's with me."

51

Another important step is to

LIVE EACH DAY WITH A DIVINE PARTNERSHIP.

You're not running your life alone now. "My *Lord* and my God," said Thomas. Lordship: rulership, mastery. We say,
"We are in partnership."
"I am doing what he wants me to do."
Finally, think about the way you breathe deeply. As you take that deep breath, the air comes in. . . . It comes into your lungs. . . . It purifies the blood that it may course through your body and make you healthy.

That's the way it is, physiologically. Every time you take a deep breath you are improving your health. And this is the way it is spiritually, too.

BREATHE GOD DEEPLY INTO YOUR LIFE.

You can breathe him into your life right now,
     and he'll purify and cleanse it. . . .
          He'll make you over again
               and make you new.
Breathing God into your life
is a very vital thing to do.
Why don't you try it now?
     Quietly, in your heart,
          welcome the living Lord.

Don't fail to meet him;
"We have seen him, and we know he lives!"
Move out of your doubts
   into an expectancy of faith,
     and say,
       "God, if you'll give me the certainty,
       I'm ready to have it. . . .
       My Lord and my God!"

Father,
   I've been a doubter and a hesitator.
     Now I trust you.
     I believe in you.
   IN PARTNERSHIP WITH YOU
   I EXPECT TO ACHIEVE GREAT THINGS
   FOR YOU.
     I am yours.
       Amen

A
REAL
CONVERSION

Zacchaeus

CONVERSION HAS TO do with changed lives and transformed people. In recent months, I've seen this change taking place in Bill Jessee, one of our members. I could have asked any of five hundred or a thousand men to tell about what God has done and what Jesus Christ means personally. I asked Bill, and this is what he said.

"Something happened to me that has really made a big change in my life and in the way I feel about everything in general. It happened recently, but it started a long time ago.

"In my twenty-six years, I have been very accident-prone. I've had surgery about eleven times for various accidents. I've been seriously burned, I've been cut, I've been shot, I've had a head-on collision on a motorcycle —you name it. I've had quite a few thrilling experiences I wouldn't like to repeat! But I've managed to come through them pretty well, and I think I'm really stronger because of that.

"I've had a sprinkling of Christian experience all through my life. I attended various churches. I've been seeking; I've been looking. I know that to accept Jesus Christ is our only salvation; this is the only answer for us and eternal life. But it goes a little bit further than that, and I just didn't find that out until recently.

"I'd been going through a struggle in the past couple of years—getting a divorce; living away from my three very young children; and working with the police department. Following the divorce I met my wife-to-be. We had the same general background. We decided that we needed a good Christian experience. We needed God in our life if we were going to make a good marriage of it. We came to Garden Grove Community Church, met several members, and decided that this was the church for us.

"Still something was lacking. We were married in the church on Thanksgiving Day. Exactly one month later, to the day, I was walking in the door, late to my work, when I slipped and fell on a waxed floor and seriously injured my back.

"I lay at home in traction for three months, then had surgery. It was unsuccessful, and for the past ten months I've been hobbling around with a cane. I was taking quite a bit of narcotics for the pain, which was so terrible I thought for a while I would have to go to crutches.

"It was one of the worst injuries I've had, and my outlook was a little dim. I went to the hospital for a second operation just one month ago and the prospects were pretty bad. They were going to do extensive surgery and the doctor wasn't too enthused about it. There was a risk of being paralyzed; there was a chance I wouldn't be able to work again, physically.

"I was in a room full of men who were nonreligious and who didn't hesitate to say so. I felt a little concerned, and I knew then what it was like to be around a bunch of men who didn't have any Christian influence in them at all. Believe me, I missed it! I knew there was something more to knowing Christ and having Christ in your life.

A Real Conversion

"Just a half hour before the operation, Gene Pearson and Harold Leestma came into my hospital room. We talked about our need for Christ and how he could really help me through. Gene Pearson was on my left; Harold Leestma was on my right. Harold Leestma prayed, and I grabbed both of their hands. There they were on either side of me, and while they were giving that prayer, I know I experienced Jesus' love coming through me, and I believe that's the Holy Spirit, and that's what it's all about.

"I know that Jesus was there in the room with us, was right there in that hospital bed with me. The Holy Spirit was what I experienced that day!

"I gave all my problems to him. I decided to stop struggling with them. I have the same problems everybody else does, but I just gave them all to Christ, and I'm going to let him handle them. I'm going to let the Holy Spirit work through me, and I'm going to profess the love of Jesus Christ to everybody I meet through my work and every place I go!

"The result of my operation, incidentally, was favorable. To the amazement of my doctor, they had nothing to do but remove a little bit of scar tissue. He just couldn't explain it to me. He thought this was fantastic! To think that that was all there was to do to my back!

"And here I am—walking without a cane. I limp a little, but I'm getting better every day. That's my story, and it's Christ who did it all for me. I know he works for me!"

Bill Jessee is a modern-day miracle.

From the Bible, I want to tell you about another miracle.

I like the story of Jesus and Zacchaeus, in the nineteenth chapter of Luke. I suppose it's because I meet so many modern-day Zacchaeuses.

The names aren't as awkward to pronounce,
or even as hard to spell.
It's usually Bill or Jim or Bob
  or Jean or Beth or Steve.
But it's the same kind of person
  walking along life's road today—
    empty,
      lonely,
        afraid—
  and then
meeting Jesus
  in some small but personal way
    and discovering a whole new life beginning.

Zacchaeus lived in the city of Jericho. It was a large and busy metropolis. It was an historic site, the place where "the walls came tumblin' down" many centuries before. Balsam trees grew in Jericho, and their fragrance permeated the atmosphere for many miles. There were groves of date palms. Traders and merchants came

60

with their caravans, crossing the Jordan River nearby. The Romans and Greeks and Arabs converged there, then went their ways—east and west, north and south.

If you were a tax collector in that thriving business center, you had a choice position because you really could make money there! This choice position belonged to Zacchaeus.

I'd like to talk to Zacchaeus as if he were a modern man.

I'd like to talk to him before he meets Jesus. . . . I meet him on the street. He's walking along toward the downtown section. Both of us have heard that Jesus is going to arrive in the city.

Zacchaeus wants to see him; so do I. I've met Jesus before. I've been following him for quite a while, but Zacchaeus has never met him. . . .

"Zacchaeus? Hello! Tell me about yourself."

Zacchaeus starts to tell me about himself. He says, "I'm a tax collector."

"I know that—and everybody else in Jericho knows it, too, of course!"

"I'm the chief tax collector of the whole area, which includes about five thousand people. I have a lot of deputies out collecting taxes, and I get a commission on everything they bring in."

I ask, "How do you become chief tax collector?"

"Well, you see, you bid on the job with the Roman government, and the highest bidder gets the job. They set a quota, and you have to meet it. Once you've met

the quota, everything above that is yours. So I'm free to
get as much as I can and as much as I want! First, meet
the quota; the rest is all profit. I can meet it in about six
to eight months if I work hard at it."

"Zacchaeus, do you think anybody really likes you
because of your job?"

"Oh, no, I guess they don't." He tries to laugh it off.
"No, not many people like me."

"Zacchaeus, you've got money and prestige. You
have influence here, really. Where are you going,
friend? Where are you going?"

"What do you mean?"

"Well, what are your long-range and short-range
goals? Where are you headed?"

"I don't know if I've really thought too much about
that. Come to think of it, I don't really think I'm going
anywhere. I don't think I'm going anywhere at all!"

"Zacchaeus, what do you really need? What do you
think you need most?"

Zacchaeus looks at me and admits honestly, "I'm
hurting, man! I'm hurting inside. I've got a lot of real
pain inside of me. You know what I need?

I need to read on someone's face,
    'I accept you.'
I need to hear a voice that says,
    'I love you.'
I need to have someone reach out a hand that shows
    me,

62

A Real Conversion

'I'll help you.'
I need to hear a challenge that tells me,
    'I need you.'
I'm hurting, I'm hurting deep inside."

So we walk along. Jesus is coming down the street. I have a couple of things I want to say to Zacchaeus before we meet this Master.

Zacchaeus looks at me and says, "Maybe you wouldn't understand."

I say, "Zacchaeus, I do understand! I do! You have five thousand people in this area, and every one of them dislikes you. And that makes you lonely, a lonely man. There are five thousand citizens around Jericho who'd like to hurt you, and you're running scared. . . . Zacchaeus, when Jesus comes by,

'TAKE A GOOD LONG LOOK AT HIM!' "

I see Jesus approaching us. Zacchaeus moves off. He's quite short and unable to see over the crowd, so he jumps up, grabs hold of the low limb of a sycamore tree, swings up on it, and has a very good view of what's going on.

What is going on? Jesus Christ is coming to Jericho. Just outside the city, says the record, he stops by the wayside. He and his disciples have been walking a long way, and many people have followed. He is tired and the disciples try to protect him. He is resting, but little children come up to him, looking at him, asking him questions—and a couple of them get up on his lap. Some mothers come and present their little children. They want Jesus to touch the children, or heal them, or let them see him.

The disciples stand as a protecting ring: "Leave him alone! He's tired. Let him rest. He's not available now!"

But Jesus says, *"Let the little children come to me! Do not stop them, because the Kingdom of God belongs to such as these"* (Luke 18:16, TEV).

After a while, they get up and walk a little further into the city. Just as they come inside the city limits, the city officials join them. Here is a man who is so respected and has so many hundreds of people around him; the whole city seems to be out to see him—and the officials want to be in on it!

So they march along with him and greet the crowd, waving to them. All of a sudden they become very embarrassed, as a blind beggar, who always sits along that road, begins to shout with a very loud voice: "Jesus? Jesus?"

Someone says, "Yes, that's Jesus, but be quiet!"

He shouts louder, "Jesus, have mercy on me!" The officials of the city try to calm him down. Someone tells him to keep still, but he won't.

Jesus stops, and the officials of the city begin to apologize: "We're very sorry. . . ."

"No, tell him to come. Tell him to come here."

A Real Conversion

And they bring the blind man to Jesus. He asks, "What do you want, friend?"

The blind beggar answers, "That I may receive my sight."

And Jesus reaches out his hand, touches his eyes, heals him, makes him see, and says, *"Your faith has made you well"* (Luke 18:42, RSV).

After that they go on into the city.

Jesus stops beneath the sycamore tree, looks up, and calls out, "Zacchaeus! Zacchaeus!"

"Yes?"

"Come down, Zacchaeus! Right away! Today I am going to your house."

I wonder if Jesus has thought that over beforehand. Or is it all spontaneous? There isn't a man in the city who likes Zacchaeus. You go to his house and you're done for! You can't associate with him and have the respect of the city.

"Zacchaeus, . . . I am going to be a guest in your home today!" (Luke 19:5, LNT).

Immediately, the fickle crowd starts to say: "He's gone to be with a man who's a sinner!"

That doesn't stop Jesus. He keeps on walking, and Zacchaeus is coming down from the tree. Zacchaeus is so surprised and startled that he drops to the ground by the base of that sycamore, leans against it for a moment, and tries to think it over: "What happened? What happened?"

Now here is where I say something more to Zacchaeus: "Zacchaeus, go with him—

'GO WITH HIM!' "

"Why? Why?"

"I'll tell you why.
He understands your deepest need . . .
   the loneliness,
     the emptiness,
      the fear.
He understands, my friend.
He cares about you.
He's the one whose voice is saying,
  'I love you.'
He's the one whose hand is reaching out,
  saying, 'I'll help you.'
He's compassionate, Zacchaeus.

"You know, you told me a little about your needs,
Zacchaeus. Jesus can meet that need—he met mine!
I haven't time now to share all the details with you,
but, believe me,

  he met me in my deepest need.
  He'll do that for you, too.
    Go with him!"

A Real Conversion

"What am I supposed to do?"
"Just receive him and believe in him!
When he goes to your house,

BELIEVE EVERY WORD HE SAYS.

Then receive what he has to offer."
"What will happen to me?"
"Some of the most wonderful things that have ever happened to anyone will happen to you!

"You're going to find joy.
    You're going to find peace.
        You're going to find a purpose in life. . . .
And one more thing, Zacchaeus,
    your deepest need. . . .
        You will be forgiven,
            and then you'll be forgiving!"

Zacchaeus went with Jesus. The unlimited love of Christ reached him, the powerful change of a real conversion took place, and a wonderful life began.

Forgiven—and forgiving!
That's for you, too.
    But don't forget this;
    it's very clear:
When Jesus came,

he looked at Zacchaeus,
   called him by name,
     and said,
"Now. . . . Come down.
I'm going to be with you today.
Now,
     Zacchaeus,
         right now. . . ."

Father,
  You are speaking to me, saying,
    "I want you.
    I want you completely—now."
I KNOW YOU CAN MEET MY DEEPEST NEED.
    I was lost; you have found me.
It is my intention
to let my life be a bright witness
to what Jesus Christ can do
with a human life.
    Help me.
      Amen

68

CONVERSION WITH A DOUBLE DIRECTION

Paul

CONVERSION ALWAYS COMES in a fresh and real way. An exciting personality whose conversion is described in the ninth chapter of Acts is called Saint Paul—but he wasn't always a saint.

He had been known by other names: Saul of Tarsus, Saul the persecutor, Paul the tentmaker, Paul the ex-convict—but not a saint. His credentials were good. He came from a good family. He was well educated. He was intelligent. He was articulate—he wrote half of the New Testament! He was ambitious, and very dedicated. But—

A saint?
He wasn't very different from the rest of us . . .
   a mortal,
     a human,
       immensely gifted . . .
   but capable of wrongdoing—
   just as anyone is.
He himself once said, *"I am the foremost of sinners"* (1 Tim. 1:15c, RSV).

The story of Saul to Paul—
   from sinner to saint—
     is the greatest conversion story in history.

First came the sudden surrender—a turning from self to God.

There were three persons who held strategic places in his surrender. One was named Stephen. Another was named Ananias. And, in between, was the person named Jesus Christ, who met him on a Damascus road.

You see, this young man Saul had legal and religious authority to go one hundred forty miles to the city of Damascus, where a colony of Christians had formed. He was to wipe them out. He went "breathing threats and murder" (Acts 9:1) in his heart. He would bring some of them to prison there and some of them to prison in Jerusalem. He was determined to get rid of Christianity.

A war was going on inside of him
  so he warred against something outside himself.
This often happens.
Someone lashes out at someone else
  because there's a lashing inside.
Saul was battling the very answer to his inner need.

Saul traveled long, hot miles. He thought he was merely on *a way*—a way to Damascus. But after he traveled it, he discovered he had been on *the Way*.

What do you think he thought about during those five or six days? Remember, he was a Pharisee, traveling with some of the Sanhedrin and some of the officials, and they couldn't talk together. They weren't in the same class.

Saul kept pretty much to himself, walking along, maybe riding on a donkey or a horse for a while, getting off again, eating his meals by himself. He had a lot of time to think!

Conversion with a Double Direction

One of the things that prompted him to think soberly was his memory of Stephen. Stephen was a heroic Christian, full of the Spirit of God. The people of Jerusalem didn't like what Stephen said about Jesus Christ. They questioned him, and he made a long and beautiful statement about God in history, moving up to that matchless event of Jesus' resurrection. Then he had a dramatic vision of the glory of God and Jesus, the living Redeemer.

At that the crowd took him outside the city and started to stone him to death.

Some of those who picked up stones found that their robes and coats were rather cumbersome, so they gave them to the care of Saul while they did the stoning. I don't know if Saul picked up any stones; but he watched Stephen die.

In a victorious spirit Stephen knelt down. His last words were, *"Lord, do not hold this sin against them"* (Acts 7:60, rsv).

Saul saw that happen.

He saw a man with a faith so strong,
 with a spirit so serene,
  with a hope so confident,
that he could die with courage, forgiving his murderers.

And all the while, on the way to Damascus, Saul kept thinking, "How do these Christians do it? What have they got? What's going on inside of them?"

73

The questions came, one after another.
Finally, a Voice seemed to be coming through—
    but he didn't want to hear it.
It seemed as if he could see something—
    but he didn't want to see it.
Then, in a unique and spectacular way, God moved
in.

A light flashed from heaven, blinding Saul. He fell
on his knees. He heard a voice: "Saul, Saul, why do you
persecute me?"
    "Who are you, Lord?"
    "I am Jesus, whom you are persecuting."
    "Lord, what do you want me to do?"

Surrender,
    conversion,
        right with God . . .
and all the background experiences of his life
were consummated in that surrender!
Tremendous! But there is more—much more!
Saul was right with God, and now he could become
Paul, a new man with a new name.
    He still needed a further experience as all of us do.
        WE NEED A CONVERSION
        WITH A DOUBLE DIRECTION.
    a turning from self to God,
      and then an outreach to the world—
        to lonely,

empty,
>self-centered lives,
learning to love them,
to give them the faith
that has brought the new life to us.
Our direction first must be upward to God,
then we must reach outward, to the world.

Saul was led by the hand into the city of Damascus. God had been there before him, and he had talked to a man by the name of Ananias.

He said, "Ananias, I have an assignment for you. You're one of my men. There's going to be a man named Saul coming here. I want—"

"Yes, I know all about him. He's put many Christians in prisons. He's even caused some to die. What do you want me to do about that?"

"I want you to go to him. . . .
>I want you to talk with him. . . .
>I want you to be his friend. . . .
>I want you to reach out in love
and show him how to live."

Ananias didn't reject the idea. He just hesitated for a moment—out of fear, perhaps, for his own life or that of his fellow Christians, who would probably be involved in this.

Then Ananias, too, surrendered.

He went down a street called Straight to the house where Saul was staying.

When Ananias saw him,
   he reached out a hand,
      and with a radiant smile said,
         "Brother Saul!"
Brother Saul . . .
   and this man Saul,
      who recently surrendered to God,
         now offered his life to the world.
This was his two-dimensional conversion.

Well, do such things happen these days? I'll give you just one illustration—I could give you many—of the way God in his purposeful providence works to turn men in his direction.

On a very busy afternoon, when I was counseling many persons in succession, I received a call that someone could not keep his two-thirty appointment. Suddenly there was a free forty-minute space in that day.

Then, just at two-thirty, a man came up the elevator to the eleventh floor and said to my secretary, "I've just got to see Reverend Leestma."

Well, that was the open time. My secretary called me, and I said, "Yes, bring him in."

He stood in front of my desk and said, "You're looking at a man who was one of the worst atheists, agnostics, and skeptics you've ever met!"

I caught the word *was*.

I said, "When did you get turned around?"

He said, "August 22."

"Oh, I know that date," I said. "Sit down and tell me about it."

He said, "I haven't believed in anything or anyone. I've gone my own way, and as far as God was concerned, I didn't know if he existed, and I couldn't have cared less.

"My wife wanted the children to go to Sunday school, and they came, sometimes. She brought them. I guess it was a little discouraging for her when I didn't help at all.

"And then, I came to church, the first Sunday of August, and sat outside in my car. You preached a sermon on *Steps to a Powerful Faith*. In the very first point you said, 'Faith is betting your life that there is a God.' "

I remembered that I had said that, wondering then about my choice of words:

"Why don't you bet your life that there is a God?

Dare to begin even though you do not know much about him.

Dare to go even though you don't know where he is going to lead you."

He said, "That appealed to me. I came back the next Sunday, and you were asking people to come two weeks later, on August 22, to a one-day Ashram—a retreat—and the leader would be E. Stanley Jones.

"E. Stanley Jones. . . . That name went through my mind. Where had I just read about him? Oh, yes. . . ."

He had picked up a book by Dale Carnegie on how to be a successful person, and in that book there was a reference to Doctor E. Stanley Jones that had appealed to him. And now he was coming here to lead an Ashram.

My friend continued, "I came at seven-thirty that Saturday morning and registered for this all-day retreat, whatever that was going to be. I came with an empty heart. At the close of the day, I had an overflowing heart."

God had reached out and touched him, through Doctor Jones and many other people here that day. I remember meeting him and talking with him for a few minutes, that's all. He was in a small-group fellowship.

That day he gave his heart to Christ. He's so turned-on for Jesus Christ today that if I were to give him a hundred jobs, he'd do them all!

You see, he experienced a conversion with a double direction:

> to Christ in a genuine surrender,
>
>> and to a world that needs such committed lives.

I tell his story because I feel that, just as in the story

of Paul, Stephen and Ananias had such a vital part
in it.

We Christians have a part in the conversion of other
people.
    Sometimes we are asked by God
        to do the impossible.
    But he gives us some incredible tools: for example,
        the tool of a forgiving, healing love—
           like Ananias's "Brother Saul!"
    That simple Christian act
        led Saul through the door to a new life.
    He stepped on the staircase of human forgiveness
        and was able to receive divine forgiveness.
    He stepped through the door
        of the heart of a man,
           and he stepped straight into
               the heart of God!
    Paul received freely, so he gave freely.

HE WAS CHANGED—AND HE BECAME LIFE-CHANGING.

He was so certain of his faith
    that he marched across the world,
        declaring such solid convictions as these:

*"He who began a good work in you will bring it to
completion"* (Phil. 1:6, rsv).

"Christ Jesus came into the world to save sinners" (1 Tim. 1:15b, RSV).

Nothing can "separate us from the love of God, which is in Christ Jesus our Lord" (Rom. 8:38, 39).

"Rejoice in the Lord always: and again I say, Rejoice" (Phil. 4:4).

And, in a prison in Rome, he wrote his final words: *"I have fought a good fight, I have finished my course, I have kept the faith: Henceforth there is laid up for me a crown of righteousness, which the Lord . . . shall give me . . . and not to me only, but unto all them also that love his appearing"* (2 Tim. 4:7, 8).

"Brother Saul" is what it hinged on. (Bless you, Ananias.)

Father,
　I NEED A CONVERSION WITH A DOUBLE DIRECTION—
　　to give my heart to Christ,
　　to give my life for his service.
　I know you will receive me.
　I know you will use me.
　　I have peace within.
　　　Thank you.
　　　Amen

Jerry's Story

On a recent Monday night, a detective from the police force called our home about ten o'clock. He said, "I'm at the county jail. I've been talking to a man named Jerry for a couple of hours. I think he's ready to start a new life, but we need some extra help. Would you be willing to talk to him?"

"Yes."

Jerry came to the phone and we talked for a while. I asked if he would come to my office the next day. He said if the officer would bail him out and come with him, he would.

So I talked to the officer again and asked him.

He said, "Tuesday is my day off."

I said, "Today is my day off, so we are even."

On Tuesday the detective came to my office with Jerry. We talked about faith, forgiveness, and Christ. I tried to be a friend. I said, "Well, we've talked for quite a while. Jerry, will you commit your life to Jesus Christ? It's the only answer. . . . I'm going to pray about it, O.K.?"

He answered abruptly, "You may if you want to."

"I do want to—and I will. You just listen. God is going to talk to you while I'm talking to him."

He looked puzzled about that. I said, "That's the way it works! I'm going to talk to him about you. You

81

listen to what he says to you when I talk to him."

He didn't say a word after my prayer—not a word. He stood up, gripped my hand, and went out. I thought I noticed a tear in his eye.

On Wednesday evening, while I was teaching a pastor's class, a call came to the office: "Jerry wants to talk to Reverend Leestma on the phone as soon as possible."

After the pastor's class I taught another class on faith sharing. It was about twenty minutes to ten by the time I came across the patio to the office to make the phone call—and Jerry was there, waiting.

He came to me excitedly. "Something's happened to me! Something new—something wonderful. I just don't know what it is—explain it to me, please. What is it?"

I said, "I can tell you what it is. Jesus Christ is entering your life, and a whole new relationship between you and God is happening. Believe it."

He said, "It's wonderful! Do you suppose we could talk to him about it?"

We were sitting in the lobby of the Tower of Hope. I said, "Yes, . . . let's go to the Chapel in the Sky."

There was no one in the chapel. We walked to the chancel, and both of us knelt. I said, "Jerry, you talk to him first."

He looked at me. "It's been so long since I've talked to him, I don't think he knows who I am . . ."

I said, "Then, I'll introduce you to him."

I did. "God, here's a friend named Jerry. He wants to meet you now. I know you're here—let him know you're here. I want you two to meet each other tonight in a very special way. Here he is. Jerry, this is God."

Jerry prayed. It was between him and God—
beautiful,
　natural,
　　with trust
　　　and surrender . . .
　　　　and a new life began
　　　　because Christ took over.

Consistently, enthusiastically, joyfully Jerry has followed a straight course on the Way. He has led his son and many others to Jesus Christ. He volunteered hundreds of hours of maintenance service to our church and was hired as an electrician on our custodial staff. His happy face is an uplift to all who see him.

He is now on a merchant ship in the South Pacific as chief electrician and is witnessing effectively to his fellow crew members. He shares his new faith in Christ at every opportunity.

His letters to me say, "Jesus is alive. He loves me. I'm sharing his love with others, just as you, Carl, Ruth, Rosemary, and so many beautiful Christians did with me. I'm not afraid because GOD IS AT MY ELBOW!"

248
Lee

CLASS   ACC.

Leestma, Harold F.

(LAST NAME OF AUTHOR)

God At My Elbow

(BOOK TITLE)

PARK CITY BAPTIST CHURCH
PARK CITY, KENTUCKY.

STAMP LIBRARY OWNERSHIP

CODE 4386-03   BROADMAN SUPPLIES
CLS-3   MADE IN U.S.A.